DAD'S MEMORABLE LANES

SADHYA KASHYAP

Contents

Acknowledgements

First and foremost, I really want to thank almighty, for the showers of blessings throughout my writing journey. I would like to express my sincere gratitude to my father and mother for their support and dedication towards me.

My father's struggles are an inspiration for me.

Further I want to thank to Notion press for giving me an opportunity to write a book.

The acknowledgements would be absolutely incomplete without the mention of Ms. Shruti Bhardwaj for all her guidance, support, and motivation throughout.

About The Author

I Sadhya Kashyap, 11 years old hails from Mohali, (PB), India. I am a seventh-grader student at St. Xavier's High School, Mohali. I enjoy spilling out my thoughts and emotions through writing. I love reading books and weaving words in poems. My writings and poetry have been published in the Times of India and anthologies. I love writing where today I'm loving to publish it in the quill house publication.

Preface

A father is the foundation of a family. No one can keep up with him. He is always there to support his family and does his best to give all the amenities he can. Every year, we celebrate Father's Day to honour our wonderful fathers for their hard work. Everyone has their own stories and sacrifices, including my father, which I'd want to share with you in this book. We all grew up hearing our parents' stories, and I am no exception. In this book, I wrote some of my father's stories as well as some letters to him. They don't communicate their emotions, but that doesn't mean they don't love us; they love us far more than we realise. My father is my bunny and my hero. And I'm my father's superstar.

Peeping into his journey

Peeping

into his

Journey

1
Student life

(Story-|)

Childhood is a period in when we are notorious and devoid of all senses. We children in this age group prefer to play rather than feel any responsibility for our studies or the mess that surrounds us.

I've never felt all of the obligations that I've ever had, but now that I'm 11, I'm starting to feel some of them. Previously, I was also too naughty and didn't bother to check on the obligations that had been assigned to me.

"I was far naughtier than you," my Father generally comments when he sees my mischief. He is used to point out the similarities between me and him all the time.

Milk is something we both enjoy. My father used to drink his glass of milk as well as his younger brother's glass of milk when he was a kid and neither told his brother nor anyone in the family .

He was so notorious that he didn't want to attend to school, so he skipped classes and spent his time playing marbles with his friends during school hours.

****

(Story-||)

One day in my father's school a spelling test was going on so the teacher gathered them in a line and started asking for spellings. My father was on 7th no. of the line. The teacher asked the Questions from the first six students about the spelling of elephant but no one knew. Next was my father's turn and he knew the correct answer. The teacher praised my father and told him to slap the rest of the wrong answered students.

My father was afraid so he slapped slowly. The teacher shouted and told him to slap hard. Then my father slapped them very hard, but that evening just after the school ended the students gathered around him and asked him "your hand is going too hard, right". That time my father gave a savage reply "If you don't want me to slap you then why don't you study and become smart enough", by saying these simple words he ran away.

****

(Story-|||)

One day my grandfather bought new shoes for my father just on 26 January morning for school republic day celebration but the shoes by mistake came small in size. What to do now in this extreme cold. Whatever, he was so dedicated to going to school that he got bare- footed to the school in the season of January.

A father inspires and admires us to go the right way, right direction and towards a right goal for our life. He never matters if I win or not. He always appreciates me even well when I try and says that I'll surely win the next time.

He always thought about my relaxation, my mind freshness and let me always go out exhaustions, overload of studies, and always want me to play after school. As a teacher he always feels that student should be out of studies after school hours.

Father's scold us but for our betterment and for the mistake that we should not ever do. We should sit with them and spend time rather than only calling them to play.

There would be many things that he wants to tell us. They would tell us stories and differences between his and our generation, time, and many other things they may tell us like my father does. I like listening to his stories.

****

2
Childhood mischieves

(Story-|)

Because they are just one year apart in age, my Father and his younger sister were both enrolled in the same class.

"Where has your brother been all these days?" my father's teacher questioned my father's sister. "What was he doing behind while not going to school?" "He leaves the house saying he's going to school, but on the way there, he starts playing marbles," sister responded. She had always supported him, but she was at a loss for words and justifications this time.

The teacher was fed up of my father's lack of concentration towards studies those days, so he dispatched a group of 7-8 boys to find my father wherever he was. The boys located my father and carried him to school with two of them holding his arms and two of them holding his legs.

My father was severely chastised by the instructor, and my father's sister complained to my grandfather at home that he used to skip school and play marbles during school hours.

My grandfather didn't say anything after my father arrived home, only said a word "I'm hearing so many complaints of yours. In present everything is going fine, but if I myself see you playing marbles or skipping school, I will not leave you," my grandfather warned.

My father continued to skip school and play marbles after that. My grandfather finally spotted him playing marbles instead of going to school one day. When my father saw that my grandfather finally saw him, he ran.

My father hid in many places but finally my grandmother and my father's sister made him hide in the trunk of wheat. After my father was caught from the wheat trunk by my grandfather, he scolded and slapped him and dared my father not to do this again.

****

(Story-||)

My father began studying ABC in the sixth grade. He once went to a city with his elder brother, and his brother's landlord asked him in which class he was studying, so to reply in English and in grace he said that he was studying in class fifty either than saying fifth.

One day my father's teacher met my father's elder brother in a city college. He noticed that my father's elder brother was so intelligent. Next day my father's teacher told father and his sister "why you both are not like your elder brother. See him and learn how well maintained he is. Tell your mother to keep you well maintained and then send you to the school every day" My father and his sister passed this same conversation to my grandfather and on that day only, my grandfather bought 4-5 sets of clothes for both, for my father and his sister and from that day my father and his sister started staying well maintained and became the monitors of the school and got reputed.

Once I also did notorious things when I was 3-4 years old like shaving off my hair with a shaver, I used to turn on the press and hide under the dining table.

Our childhood is all about our notorious things that we dare to pursue. Our fathers tell us their childhood stories and the things that they dared to persue, their struggles, their moments inspire us to be more than they themselves are and keeps us away from the mistakes that they had made. The facilities that we are getting today are all due to there hard work, dedication, tolerance power, and his patience leads to whatever he is today.

There are so many similarities between my father and me as a daughter. Father's are the best friends of daughter's. He also tells me the difference between his and my generation, his living style, and all the facilities I'm getting. They used to go on cycles in his generation, but now we have cars, scooters, and bus facilities to go to school.

How much they struggled in their life. They have only not struggled but they are still struggling. They don't let us a pinch of a mischievous thing that has ever come to our life and never let something wrong comes our way.

****

(Story-||||)

In childhood we all do naughtiness as it's our age, so do my father did in his childhood. So, I'm going to tell you about my father in his childhood.

In his childhood he used to graze the cows and sing songs in his fields. He used to tease the old people by singing songs. Old people get irritated very fast so he used to do this thing. He used to sing the song "बहुतदेरसेदरपेआँखेंलगीथी, हज्जूरआते-आतेबहुतदेरेकरदी।". He also used to dance and tease the old people.

My father always used to hit the children standing there on the road. He used to hit them a lot. To whom he hits, that children complaints to his grandfather. My father's grandfather was blind so he could not see anything. My father's grandfather took a stick of wood to hit my father. The children showed grandfather the way and the grandfather used to become a ball of fire. So, here you see my father's naughtiness. We children's today also do some of these things like naughtiness; just there is a difference between the facility we get and what they got.

****

3

Dreams

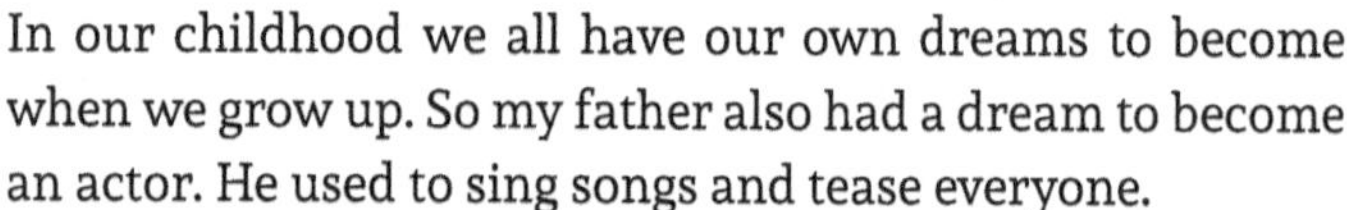

In our childhood we all have our own dreams to become when we grow up. So my father also had a dream to become an actor. He used to sing songs and tease everyone.

In his village everyone usually call him by his nick name "Billu" and he had his famous dialogue "Action aur reaction se bharpur vada...... Billu Dada...."

He wanted Ratti Agnihottri to play his mother role if he enters the film line. He is very fond of movies and likes thriller movies a lot.

The first movie that he saw in theater was Jai Santoshi Maa. He used to purchase the low price front seat movie tickets and sit at the high priced balcony seats.

During my father's kid life he was very naughty and my grandmother was very tired of seeing his naughtiness so, one day my grandmother gave my father's cousin 75 paisa (12 aane) who was studying in 5th class to register his name in the school.

Once my father's friend's brother died so his parents told my father to keep the friend with him. My father's friend started living with my father. After some time the friend told my father that he wanted to study. So, my father said"ok, you could give the exam for the air force". The friend gave the exam and he got selected. My father got reputed in the whole village and the friends' parents told that their son got selected in the air force just because of my father.

****

4

Actor in Him

Some people always dream to be an actor in their childhood, so do my father. My father always wanted to be an actor in his childhood. My father always liked to watch thrillers and fighting movies.

The movies of Sunny Deol inspired him a lot to be an actor. He always wanted to be an actor like him. As I told you that he wanted Ratti Agnihottri to play his mother if he entered the film line and he was very fond of movies as he liked thriller movies a lot and he is a fond of movies now too.

My father is a teacher, a mathematician. Being an actor is not so easy. Just because of some issue of money he left his dream to be an actor, and just with a bit of money he became a mathematics teacher. Whatever, now he is a great mathematician and he has to continue. His hard work led him to his mountain of success as it was waiting for him for a long time. He did so much to have his success.

****

5

Journey towards his goals

"HARD WORK LEADS TO SUCCESS:

My father was living in Roorkee with his elder brother. After his +2 his elder brother was shifted to a new city and my father was alone in Roorkee.

He had only 2 options: he had to stay in Roorkee or he needed to go back to his village. He wanted to stay in Roorkee but he doesn't have money for his expenses. The only option was to go back to his village.

So, for the money he started teaching tuitions. He worked very Hard. He goes house to house to take tuitions. He started teaching Mathematics as up to his elder brother who was also a mathematician field.

After passing +2 he started taking coaching of upto +2 classes when passed Bsc 1st year he started taking the coaching of upto +1, +2 classes and when he passed Bsc 2nd year he started taking tuition of Bsc 1st year also and after he passed Bsc final year (3rd year) he started tuitions of +1, +2, Bsc 1st year, 2nd year and Bsc final year (3rd year).

****

(Story-||)

When my father was in 10th class his elder brother used to take tuition of Bsc students. So, he made him sit with the students of Bsc to learn.

He would not understand the concepts as being a student of 10th and sitting with the students of Bsc feels a bit difficult to understand the concepts.

But when my father was in BSc, he remembered those concepts a bit thoroughly. His hard work helped him with his expenditure. Thus now he is a great mathematics teacher. He worked so hard and I don't think I can ever do like him.

****

(Story-|||)

When my father tried for BSc admission in a reputed college of Roorkee but by that time admissions were already closed. So, he talked to his elder cousin brother and took admission in a village college far from Roorkee, where students never prefer to take admission. He studied well and scored good marks in BSc 1st year. On the basis of that marks, he was able to transfer his admission in BSc 2nd year onwards to the reputed college of Roorkee where he wanted to take admission in 1st year.

After completing BSc he wanted to do MSc from IIT Roorkee, so he thought of giving the JAM exam to take the admission. While going to the JAM entrance examination centre, my father's friend was riding the bicycle and sitting at the front my father was revising his notes for the entrance exam. As he couldn't take the notes inside the examination centre, he kept them in the bushes. He worked so hard for the achievement. When he came out of the center and searched the notes in the bushes he never found them again.

He got selected on an all India basis and was offered the top specialized branch of MSc in Industrial Mathematics and Informatics at IIT Roorkee.

****

(Story-|V)

When he was in BSc 1st year he didn't have books to practice and learn, so he would ask his friends for their books for some time to study.

He used to ask the notes that they use to write while there tuitions and my father note them and study self and also make his tuition students understand.

My father knew the time of the walk of his friend's tuitions teacher so if he had any doubt in the notes he used to meet the teacher and used to ask his doubts.

The exam came and he didn't have a book to study. He waited for his friend to complete their studies and give the books to my father. He waited a lot but the friend was not able to give his book to my father.

That day my father bought a book on rent for a day for ?10 and gave the book after studying and the exam.

Even one day my father was in MSc he mostly skipped his classes after lunch as he had given that time to his coaching students. His teacher scolded him for not attending the classes after lunch, my father apologized for that and tried to manage it.

During MSc he gave complete coaching and after MSc he was selected for lecturer in Mathematics to the students of BCA and BSC at Institute of management studies (IMS) Roorkee which was affiliated with HNB University, Srinagar Garhwal (Uttrakhand).

****

(Story-V)

One day, a staff of IIT Roorkee asked my father to give home tuitions to his daughter studying in BSc final. My father agreed and started to that girl and her friends. The girl gave JAM exam and got selected for MSc Applied Mathematics at IIT Roorkee. Her parents praised my father a lot, that just because of him their daughter got selected in IIT Roorkee and gave him so much gifts like clothes, watch etc.

During his MSc my father was selected in the Center for Aeronautical Studies and Analyses, DRDO Bangalore, Karnataka, for summer industrial training, which was a mandatory training course of his degree but he didn't have enough money to travel from Roorkee to Bangalore. So my father's friend Mr. Avdhesh gave my father his tuition fees to complete his summer training. Then he travelled from Roorkee to Bangalore in a sleeper compartment for three days without reservation.

After reaching there he searched for many rooms to spend the night but he doesn't have enough money for the room rent so he took a room in dharamshala near railway station at a low price that he can afford.

From the dharamshala, the office of DRDO (Defense Research & development organization) was too far. The staff of the DRDO office was supportive and helpful. In the office there was a tea server who offered my father a room in his house for rent at a very low price that he could afford.

Two months ago my father's summer training was about to be over. The tea serving uncle told my father that his family is going to come today and we'll have a party. The tea server's uncle's family reached. They made a special dish for my father. My father asked their children what dish have been prepared today. They said "Mutton". My father asked them 'what this mutton is' as he never heard this word about. They replied, "It's the flesh of a goat". But my father was a vegetarian. So he told them that he doesn't eat mutton and is a vegetarian. Then they served him sambar and rice.

The training was over and my father got a scholarship in industrial training as a stipend of ?2000 Per month.

****

(Story-V|)

One day my father scolded a girl student who was attending his coaching classes. My father asked her, "Where are your parents working?"She quietly said that "they are running an institute". "Which institute" my father asked. She hesitated and said "sir the institute in which you are working". My father was shocked "what! My boss daughter is taking coaching from me". It was a shocking and proud moment for him. She said "yes sir, that's why I never told you about it". After some time he left this job as he wanted to continue M Phil in Mathematics.

****

(Story-V||)

In the middle of last semester of M Phil my father started searching for a job. He didn't know how to apply for jobs. My father's friend told my father that "check the Hindustan news paper on Tuesday and Times of India on Wednesday as in it vacancies are getting published on these days" his friend suggested him. So he started applying.

He applied for 2-3 jobs. He was afraid of why any offer was not coming, so his friend told him that "apply for just about 10 jobs, in any 2 you will be selected" his friend suggested him.

My father applied for about the 10 best jobs in India. My father got an offer to give an Interview in Scindia school, it is one of the best boys schools in India. My father reached there and gave his interview. He got selected but they told him that "why are you applying for this job, you are MPhil from IIT Roorkee. Your profession is some other, you don't deserve this job, and you should take a job in a university".

My father was appreciated as it was the best school in India and the principal words mean a lot to him. After that he also got job offers of job for interview from a college in Dehradun and Chitkara Institute.

****

(Story-VIII)

As my father got an interview letter late from Chitkara head office Chandigarh so he first gave an interview in one college in Dehradun and started working there.

First he liked that college and worked there for a week. After that he also thought of trying giving the interview in Chitkara Institute. He and his four friends from Roorkee also gave interviews at Chitkara.

His two friends got a call for a second round interview from Chitkara Institute and were preparing to leave for Chandigarh. My father thought that he should ask whether he is also selected for the second round of interview or not, so he called Mr. Mohit Chitkara (Vice Chairman of Chitkara Institute) at 9:30 PM to confirm.

Mr. Mohit Chitkara replied that Mr. Ashok Pal, you are shortlisted for the second round of interview which is scheduled tomorrow at 12:30 PM and the letter for the interview call is already dispatched. But my father didn't receive any letter due to a postal delay. Next morning he had to leave for Chandigarh for an interview but the main problem was that he didn't have money to travel and it was too late to ask from someone. Though it was the weekend and his friends had left for their homes.

It was not possible for him to arrange money as the day was too rainy. So he decided not to go for an interview. In the morning when he woke up again, the interview struck his mind, it was raining heavily.

He was continuously thinking what to do, the time was running out and the train from Roorkee to Chandigarh was also over. Now he has to travel by bus which is too costly but the interview was going through his mind.

Then he saw a shop near his house had opened, he thought to ask money from that shopkeeper to go for an interview but his image was not good in the area, he was considered as a rude man. My father desperately wanted to go for an interview so he managed to ask for money from that uncle. After knowing the reason why my father wanted money, he gave it to him instantly. Likewise my father managed to go for an interview at Chitkara Institute, his shoes and clothes were totally wet.

Whatever the situation was, he got selected. He was praised a lot and was one of the best teachers in that Institute and worked there for 6 years. He moved further to complete his PhD and now he is a true mathematician. His hard work led him to his mountain.

It's not enough yet for him. He did so much hard work and now he is getting the fruit of his efforts. Father's are the best. They are providing us with all the facilities that they had never got in their childhood. It's like they are completing their happiness by giving us. Thank you to the entire father's in the world for what they are doing for us.

****

Letter's from his loving daughter

Letter's

From his loving

Daughter

6
My 8th birthday

Dear Dad,

I still remember how you celebrated my eighth birthday, and I'm grateful to you for that. My birthday was just as fantastic as you. It was the best day of my life. It was full of surprises and shocking revelations. The doll cake was unexpected at first. When I saw it, my mouth widely opened.

Mom had shown me a doll cake on a website before my birthday, but I hadn't expected it. You guys went at market around 10 p.m on the 12th night, so I expected of a cake, but I didn't expected a doll cake. All the things were just out of my expectations.

When I woke up at 12:00 a.m., my bed was cluttered of gifts. I felt so much weight on me that when I opened my eyes, I saw that my bed was decorated with balloons and that I was fully covered with gifts on me which took me a while to get up from bed, every moment was fascinating. I didn't expect anything before this day, but after the night, it was completely unexpected. Now I realise how much you've done for me and I'm so thankful

You worked as hard as you could, Dad. You do everything for me and are always concerned with my comfort. Everything you do is for us. Papa, you are wonderful, and I owe you a thousand thanks. Yes, the narrative isn't over yet. So I went to school that day, and everyone wished me.

Gifts and cards were also sent to me by a friend. This was an incredible day. After that, my mother and you forced me to take a half-day off and go on a tour of a garden and chokhi dhani. It was incredible. All of the magic tricks they demonstrated, walking on a rope were enthralling, and I sincerely thank you from the bottom of my heart.

I just don't know how to express my gratitude for everything you've done for the things that I never expected.. And now we're off to the garden. It was lush with greenery and a variety of plants I had never seen before. It was a great time, and I completely forgot to mention the puppet show in Chokhi Dhani. It was hilarious.

We also went camel riding there. We stayed there until 9:00 p.m., and I was exhausted by the end of the night. After returning home, I promptly dozed off. I can't tell you how grateful I am for everything you've done for me. This was a once-in-a-lifetime opportunity for me, and I will never forget it.

I may not be able to express my emotions, but trust me when I say that the day my father created for me and I say in my heart that this day was fascinating, amazing, and everything else I can think of.

!You have created the best and the most excellent day of my life!

ᗷᗷᗷ

7
City of dreams

Dear Dad,

I remember when we were looking for a house near Chandigarh and we discovered a lot and I loved a society called City of Dreams but you thought for a society that looked better than this one but I was pressuring you to purchase it. And you may recall that after you returned from work, I would say to you that dear papa "Sapno ka shehar to sapna hi reh jayenge,"

You know I forced you a lot and I was scolding you that "why are you looking another society where this is the best in all of them" I really liked the society never looked after it., when you ask me for any other society I would say no even if I have liked it or not I would choose this city of dreams only well I felt it that it was the best.

"I liked it but I'm looking for some other societies that are just for reference. Don't worry I'll buy it, just look at others if you like any more than this" my father used to say. I replied "I don't like any of the society more than this and why a need of a reference when you got the best choice.

I used to say and after saying this whole paragraph of "Ooh, what to do" I used to say myself in an irritating and frustrating voice because I was not able to understand why you were not buying it.

That time I was 7 or 8 years old so I realized today that I did not understand what you wanted to say and was taking it in the wrong way. Finally, after forcing you a lot you finally purchased that house.

I was too happy and they said that they'll giving the possession by December 2018 but they didn't gave till and in December 2018 the house was just was made up of brick and postponed to next year after 6months and then again 2019 December and then due to rain they postponed the possession date to December 2020 and I was eagerly waiting and again due to corona virus again postponed to the next year 2021.

I was not able to understand why they are not giving the possession and why isn't the house ready yet, does it take this much time to prepare just a small ground floor house but finally they gave the possession in march 2021 and got the keys into our hand finally.

I finally understand how much you sacrificed for my satisfaction and my comfort. I'm so thankful to you for all you have done for me and I can realize how much I have disturbed you for me to fulfill all my wishes and neither giving importance to anything after my wishes.

Father, I'm so thankful for all your support and all the things for which you have encouraged me. You are the one who helped me to stand up here.

!Thank you for everything father!

8

Walked upon my interest

Dear Dad,

You have really always walked upon my interest. You have always been by my side. You always encouraged me and led me to this stage to write a book. I always made you dance on my fingers and I'm doing it till now. Father, I remember when my mother used to hit me after coming from the office and used to ask me "did mom hit you a lot" I replied "Nah dad, she just got a bit over confident" I used to reply.

Father you may remember that when I was small I used to command my grandfather upto myself. If I told him to stand up and dance onto the bed he used to stand and do everything as per me. He never scolds me whether it's right or wrong for him and just does whatever I say. Father I feel Grandfather's are just like father's for me like you know grandpa was like a toy for me. Father all you did for me I'm so thankful and I know father's are the best like you.

Father the only thing I would like to ask you is how could you sacrifice for everything, don't you have your own dreams. I am really confused how you can let your dreams go and look up for me. I think I can't be like you, if I can be then how I don't know. Father, how much hard work you have done in your life, I can't just believe it.

Father, all you have done in your life to reach here is fascinating. The story from your childhood to today your success has inspired me and will inspire everyone. How you have done everything without any facility.

Now I know, father you are the best, father you are the best friends of your daughter's, father you provide everything you could. I feel it's too difficult for me to reach a position like you. Father you are a precious gem of nature heavenly gifted, thank you for everything father you have done for me.

!You are the brilliant person in my life!

♭♭♭

9
Family time

Dear Dad,

You and I have spent so much time with each other and we'll continue to spend even more time together. We usually go on a tour during my exams. Yeah it's true, you might not take us out usually are going on you may not take us out usually but you surely take me while my paper.

While when you plan and I say that "father' my papers going on, I have to prepare" so, you would say "your papers are going the whole year and now it's family time. One time you'll get low marks but not the other time". You never worried about my papers marks because I know because you do this if I get over tension. You always do about my relaxation. And now just because of your confidence I never fear about papers. I feel relaxed and out of tension while my paper's announcement comes.

!Your motivation just led me to this small success!

ﻉﻉﻉ

10
my childhood

Dear Dad,

I really remember when you used to tell me the stories of my naughtiness when I was small and I also remember how you entertained me in my childhood.

You entertained me by singing my favorite songs, such as la la la, chanda hai tu mera, and a song based on the names that everyone calls me. Father, you've always managed to keep me entertained at every split second. I memorize that you made me sit on your stomach and sing songs for me. For me, your tummy was like a cushion, and I loved sitting on it. I still like to sit on your stomach. When I was younger, I remember that I used to sit on your tummy and obstruct your way so that you would pay attention to me and play with me when you were watching TV and not paying attention to me. If you're still not paid attention I would start hitting on your stomach.

!Father, you are the best entertaining character for me!

🝑🝑🝑

11
Holi Celebration

Dear Dad,

I recall how you used to make my Holi day a wonderful occasion for me. You and mother would first go to the market and buy pichkaris that I wouldn't imagine, unique pichkaris. Father, you always work your butt off to make my every day special, and you also go out of your way to make my holidays memorable. It's a one-of-a-kind creation every time you build it.

You would specifically address the men who play dhole for me, and I would dance. Father, you are the most entertaining person I have ever met. Though everyone's fathers are the finest, I mean fathers are the best like you, you are the best in the world. You make sacrifices and do everything for the sake of everything. Thank you, Father, for providing me with every convenience you have never had.

!Thank you for everything!

🖤🖤🖤

12
For my schooling

———❤———

Dear Dad,

I now realise how much you have given up to provide me with the greatest educational opportunity possible. You attempt to get the best you can afford whenever you buy something for me for everything, you make the best decision you can.

I recall you considering the Air Force as a possible school for me while you were deciding on choosing a school. Mom completed the selection form since you liked it. They set a day for going to school and check the list of selected students.

We went to the school to examine the selection list when the deadline arrived. When we arrived, we discovered that the date had been rescheduled for another three days.

You looked at the dress of the students that they were wearing and you didn't like it. You also heard that the teachers of the school were also that much qualified, so you just took this school out of your mind and never looked after it. You even didn't check the list after. So father, I thank you for giving me a great platform. You never look for the necessity you need, but always mine look for me.

Thank you...!

♡♡♡

13

Traveling to mumbai

Dear Dad,

It's been a long time since we've taken a journey to Mumbai on a regular basis. We lived there for 6 months throughout this epidemic as well. You accomplished everything for my pleasure, and I owe you a debt of gratitude. You have done and continue to do so much for me. Where is my happiness, there you go.

We also got a tour to Mumbai's Barvi Dam during this period. We visited numerous destinations in Mumbai before 2-3 years, including Marine Drive, Siddhivinayak Temple, Dadar Beach, Barbeque Restaurant, and others. Marine Drive's ice cream is something I genuinely miss.

The ice cream was incredible. My mouth is always tingling with the flavours of Black Current, chocolate, and vanilla. And the barbeque meal was very delicious. "WOW!" I exclaimed as the roasted corns entered my tongue. Father, thank you for everything you're doing for me. You're the greatest. You are the rhythm of my heart. You are a fantastic father.

!I really thank you from depth of my heart!

ᘐᘐᘐ

14

Trip to Rishikesh And At war with Corona

Dear Dad,

You may recall that mamu and mami visited Punjab this year, and we were treated to a trip to Rishikesh because mami was seeing North India for the first time. You may recall that when we arrived in Rishikesh, we were given an ashram to reside in along the Ganga. We can feel the fresh air on our faces if we go to the house's balcony. It's a pleasant sensation.

After that, we considered going to Nilgiri to see the Nilkanth Temple. We arrived, parked the car, and now must walk a distance of around 2 kilometres. It was suffocatingly packed.

We considered returning. We then decided that we had travelled too far and that we would leave after completing the darshan.

Mamu gets a fever after returning to Punjab, and we tested him positive. We were isolated when he tested positive, but you were still quite concerned about me. Father, I appreciate your thoughtfulness.

❥❥❥

15
Sincere Apology

Dear Dad,

Father, please accept my heartfelt apologies for everything. Please accept my apologies if I have to apologise to you several times.

There were probably a hundred things for which I should have apologised, but I didn't. So, please accept my apologies and my gratitude for this chance. Now I'm here to thank you for everything you've done for me.

I'm very sorry for all the awful things I've done with you, for all the misbehaviour I've done that I never knew about or that you never notified me about, and now you've forgotten about it, and I'm thankful for all the services you give.

I owe you a huge debt of gratitude and apologise for everything. I've messed up with you.. Thank you very much, papa. In my opinion, you are the best father. Thank you very much.

!Love you!

My Cutie Bunny

***The last but not the least I just want to dedicate this short
poem on my dearest, loving father or my cutie bunny***

Papa, Papa
I love u, I love u
You are the one
Who is the best
You are my hero
You are my life
You are my buddy
You are my bunny
You are my affection of love
You are my happiness
And I know you love me
You are the one
Who is the best
You are the ray of sun
Who keep me temperate in winter
Chill in summer
I really love you bunny
You are a mountain pop
You will attain upto height of Mount Everest
You are the one
Who is the best
Papa, Papa
I love u, I love u